THE
ORIGIN
AND
EARLY HISTORY
OF THE
𝕽𝖚𝖘𝖘𝖎𝖆 𝖔𝖗 𝕸𝖚𝖘𝖈𝖔𝖛𝖞 𝕮𝖔𝖒𝖕𝖆𝖓𝖞,

TAKEN FROM

HAKLUYT, PURCHAS,
ETC. ETC.

LONDON:

1830.

In the interest of creating a more extensive selection of rare historical book reprints, we have chosen to reproduce this title even though it may possibly have occasional imperfections such as missing and blurred pages, missing text, poor pictures, markings, dark backgrounds and other reproduction issues beyond our control. Because this work is culturally important, we have made it available as a part of our commitment to protecting, preserving and promoting the world's literature. Thank you for your understanding.

THE ORIGIN AND EARLY HISTORY

OF THE

RUSSIA OR MUSCOVY COMPANY.

THE names of Cabot or Cabota are so interwoven with the Origin and History of the Russia Company, that a reference to the services and merits of these celebrated navigators, as connected with British discovery, and the opening of a trade between Great Britain and Russia, becomes a subject of curiosity and great interest. In the reign of Henry the Seventh, John Cabot, a Venetian, settled at Bristol, offered his services to this monarch, who commissioned him and his sons—Lewis, Sebastian, and Sanches, to discover unknown lands. In the year 1497, they discovered Newfoundland, and afterwards the Continent of America. Henry the Eighth succeeded his father, Henry the Seventh, but he so little encouraged such enterprises that, Sebastian Cabot, finding his services disregarded, offered them to

1497.

the Court of Spain, where they were joyfully accepted; and so successful were they, that he discovered the River de la Plata and made several fortunate voyages for that Government.

1553. On the succession of Edward the Sixth, Sebastian Cabot returned into the service of England, and in 1553, waited on the young king with a plan for attempting a N.E. passage to China and the East Indies. Sebastian Cabot was, at this period, so advanced in years, being about seventy-six, that he could not himself undertake the voyage, but he made the plan, drew the outline, and prepared the instructions for the expedition, which was undertaken at the expense and risk of a society of merchants who called themselves " The Mystery and Company " of Merchant Adventurers for the Discovery of " Regions, Dominions, Islands and places un- " known."

The capital of this Company was £6000, divided into shares of £25 each, which entitled the subscriber to be a member of the Company. Sebastian Cabot, having been the prime mover in the undertaking, was chosen to be the Governor. The expedition consisted of three vessels:—

The Bona Esperanza   ..120 tons..Sir Hugh Willoughby.
The Edward Bonaventura 160 ,, ..Richard Chancellor.
The Bona Confidentia .. 90 ,, ..Cor. Darforth.

Edward the Sixth patronized the undertaking

in every possible way, and gave a letter, written in different languages, recommending the expedition to the sovereigns of the countries they might discover or touch at.

On the 10th of May, the expedition sailed from Gravesend, and when off the North Cape a storm separated the vessels. Sir Hugh Willoughby, with two of the three ships, put into a harbour in Lapland, where himself and party were frozen to death. Richard Chancellor, in the Edward Bonaventura, pursued his voyage, and, having entered a large bay, discovered a fishing boat, the people of which came on board and informed Chancellor that the Bay was called St. Nicholas, belonging to a country called Russia, or Muscovy. Chancellor proceeded overland to Moscow, and, on presenting the letter of Edward to the Czar, or Emperor Iwan Basiliewich, was well receeived, and it must, in justice to Chancellor, be acknowledged that he first discovered the way to Archangel, and established that amicable intercourse and profitable commerce which has continued for so many years. 1553.

The Emperor received Chancellor with great distinction, inviting him to his court; and, on his leaving, gave him a letter of recommendation, addressed to the King of England. Chancellor, on his return to England, finding that Edward was dead, delivered the Emperor's letter to Philip and Mary, who, on his return, on a second voyage, 1554.

furnished him with a letter to the Czar, requesting for the Company privileges, liberties, and powers of trading. To this Company Philip and Mary granted a charter to the Marquis of Winchester, Earl of Arundel, and the different officers of state—to different gentlemen and merchants, &c. by the name of " Merchant Adventurers for the Discovery of Lands, Territories, Isles, Seigniories unknown ;"—and in consideration that Sebastian Cabot had been the chiefest setter forth of the voyage, he was appointed, for life, the Governor ; and four Consuls and twenty-eight Assistants were further appointed, but whose election was to take place every year.

The Russia Company, not possessing any documents relative to these early discoveries, it is probable they were destroyed at the fire of London,—copies, however, and all particulars are fortunately to be found in " Richard Hak-
" luyt's Collections of Navigations, Voyages,
" and Discoveries," first published in 1599. In his preface to the reader, he writes of the Russia or Muscovy Company. " Next under the Title
" of the North and Northwestern Voyages, you
" will find the old Northern Navigators of our
" British Kings, &c.; and, next to them in con-
" sequence, the discoveries of the Bay of St.
" Nicholas, the Colmogro, the Pechora, the Isles
" of Waigats, of Nova Zembla, and of the Sea,
" eastward, towards the River Ob; after that, the

"opening, by Sea, of the Great Dukedom and
"Empire of Russia, with the notable and
"strange journey of Master Jenkinson to Boghar,
"in Bactria, whereunto you may add six voyages,
"eleven hundred wersts up against the stream
"of the Dwina to Vologda, then 180 wersts by
"land to Yaroslaw, on the mighty Volga; then
"hence 2500 wersts down the stream to the
"ancient Mart Town of Astrachan, and so to the
"manifold Mouths of the Volga; and thence by
"ship over the Caspian Sea into Medea; and
"further thence, also, with camels, into Georgia,
"Armenia, Hyrcania, Gallas, and the chief
"towns of Persia, whereunto the Company of
"Muscovy Merchants, to the perpetual honour
"of the City and Company, have performed
"more than any one, yea, than all the nations of
"Europe besides."

Hakluyt's collection of voyages only went to the end of the fifteenth century; but had he continued them some years later, in noticing the services rendered to the state by the Russia Company, he would have added, that most important service and advantage to Great Britain, the establishing the whale-fishery to Greenland, by the Company, which was effected in the year 1610.

In noticing the great and important services rendered to the state, by the Russia Company, it is due to the originator and first Governor of the

Russia Company to give more at length the narrative of his life. Sebastian Cabot, the first Governor of the Russia Company, was born at Bristol, (and, therefore, a British born subject and Englishman,) in the year 1477; he was the son of John Cabot, a Venetian, who, in 1495, obtained, from Henry the Seventh, Letters Patent, under the great seal, empowering him and his three sons to discover unknown countries; but it was not till the spring of 1497, that these bold adventurers sailed from Bristol, with the view of discovering a northwest passage to India. In this voyage they discovered Newfoundland, in another they discovered that part of the Continent of North America, which has since been called Florida. By a letter which was extant at the time of Hakluyt, written, by Sebastian Cabot, to a friend, it appears that John Cabot, the father, was dead, when this voyage was undertaken, so that the discovery of the country, afterwards called Florida, was made by Sebastian Cabot. Thus, the discovery of the Continent of America was not due to Columbus, who was unaquainted with it till a year after this voyage, but to Sebastian Cabot, who commanded and directed the expedition which led to the discovery of this vast Continent. In 1517, Sebastian Cabot sailed for the East Indies; but, after touching on the Coast of Brazils, he arrived at Porto Rico and Hispaniola, where he carried on some trade, and then shaped his course to England. After this he entered the service of Spain, sailed from Cadiz to the Cape de Verd Islands, and on this voyage discovered the Rio de la Plata, Salvadore, and Paraguay,—he remained on the coast a considerable time; but, being disappointed in his expectations, he returned to England in 1531.

In the reign of Edward the Sixth he had a pension settled on him as Grand Pilot of England, in which character and situation he planned the expedition which led to the discovery of St. Nicholas, and opened the intercourse between Russia and Great Britain. Sebastian Cabot was the first who discovered the variation in the compass.

The Russia Company, being now established by charter, sent out a second expedition in the year 1555; it consisted of two ships—the Bonaventura and another—under the direction of Richard Chancellor; and the Company appointed George Killingworth, Henry Lane, and Richard Prince to be agents or factors to the Company. Chancellor was furnished with a letter from Philip and Mary to the Czar. On arriving at St. Nicholas they proceeded to Moscow, where, as before, they were well received. The Emperor granted the Company very considerable advantages and privileges: they, as before, were invited to dine; and Killingworth must have been peculiarly acceptable to the Russians, who wore

1555.

their beards, for the Czar, at dinner, held Killingworth's beard across the table, gave it to the Metropolitan, who said, in Russ, " This is God's gift." His beard is described as thick, broad, of a yellow colour, and in length five feet and two inches. Killingworth, being informed that some Russian fishermen had discovered the bodies of Sir Hugh Willoughby and his party, sent thither, and recovered part of the property and the will of Sir Hugh, by which it would appear the party lived till January, 1554. Through their able negotiations and good conduct the Czar granted the Company great privileges to Sebastian Cabot, as Governor; Sir George Barnes, &c. as Consuls; and Sir John Gresham, &c. as Assistants. Chancellor returned the same year, bringing with him a letter from the factor Killingworth, giving a long detailed account of the state of trade in Russia, the kind reception of the party by the Emperor, and the different privileges granted to the Company. So anxious was the Russia Company to follow up the attempt to discover a N.E. passage to India, that, in 1556, they sent out a small vessel, under Stephen Burroughs, to discover the river Ob. On arriving at the straits of Wagatz, he found so much ice that, the season being greatly advanced, he returned to Colmogro, where he wintered, and, in the following year (1557), was ordered to Wardhuis, in Norway,

1556.

to seek the Bona Esperanza and Confidentia. In 1556, the Company sent out a third expedition; the Edward Chancellor and the Philip and Mary. On his return, the same year, Chancellor brought with him, in his vessel, the Edward, a Russian Ambassador, Osep Nepeoff, with sixteen followers, with rich presents to the Queen. The Edward (in which was the Ambassador and Chancellor) was shipwrecked on the coast of Scotland, and the excellent commander (Chancellor), in his anxiety to save the Ambassador, was himself drowned. The cargo, consisting in wax, train oil, furs, and tallow, valued at £20,000, was entirely lost. The Russia Company, on learning the calamity, sent down two of their body to compliment the Ambassador, and to render him every assistance in their power. The Ambassador, with the party, arrived in London in February, 1557; he was there received by eighty Russia merchants, all richly apparelled, and all having chains of gold about their necks, their servants, in great numbers, in rich and uniform liveries, and well mounted. They conducted him to a merchant's house, within four miles of London, where he remained that night. In the mean time, a proper riding-habit was prepared for him. The next morning the Russia Company, in great numbers and great state, conducted him towards London. By the way he was met by the Lord Viscount Montague, attended by numerous knights, squires, and gentlemen, to the number of three hundred persons; near the city, four of the Russia Company, richly apparelled, presented him with a stately gelding, 1557. which he mounted. At Smithfield he was met by the Lord Mayor and Court of Aldermen. King Philip, returning from Flanders, the Ambassador was received in great state by the King and Queen. The Ambassador dined with the Russia Company, at Drapers' Hall, when a cup of wine being drank to him, he was requested to allow the Company to pay his expenses from his arrival in England to his departure from Gravesend. In May, after receiving letters from Philip and Mary, he embarked at Gravesend. The ship Philip and Mary arrived safe in the year 1557, after having encountered many dangers. The expedition which carried back the Ambassador consisted of four ships, and were commanded by Master Anthony Jenkinson, namely, The Primrose, Jenkinson, in which was the Ambassador; John the Evangelist; Anne; and The Trinity.

The expedition arrived, without accident, at St. Nicholas; and Jenkinson, on his arrival at Moscow, was received with great distinction by the Emperor. This was the last expedition made by the Russia Company in this reign.

One of the principal objects of the Russia Company being to discover a route to China, either by land or sea, Anthony Jenkinson, according to the instructions he had received from the Company, left Moscow on the 23d April, 1558, having obtained, from the Czar, letters to the divers kings and princes through whose territories he might pass. In July he arrived at Astrachan; and, in August, he entered the Caspian Sea, crossing which, and making a long land journey with camels, he arrived at Boghar, in Bactria, in December. Bactria, which had belonged to Persia, was then governed by an independent king, who received Jenkinson with great kindness. Boghar was the great mart for merchants, who brought their goods in large caravans from India, Persia, Russia, and China. Jenkinson passed the winter in Boghar; and, in the spring of 1559, returned by the route he came, and, in September, arrived at Moscow. The Emperor again received him with great attention, and graciously accepted the presents he offered, namely, a white cow's tail from China, and a drum from Tartary, and received courteously the different ambassadors, whom Jenkinson had brought with him from different countries through which he had passed. He dined with the Emperor, who asked him many questions concerning the countries he had visited on this journey. After passing the winter in

1558.

1559.

Moscow, he was allowed to depart in the spring of 1560, and arrived at Colmogro in May, and in England the end of the year.

1560.

The Russia Company, with that spirit of enterprise which characterized all their proceedings, determined on sending out Jenkinson to pursue their favourite object—to discover a passage, either by land or sea, to China. For this purpose they requested from Queen Elizabeth, who was then on the throne, letters to the Emperor of Russia, requesting license and safe conduct for Anthony Jenkinson to pass through his empire of Russia into Persia to the Great Sophy; and, further, letters to the Sophy of Persia, requesting permission to trade, &c. Queen Elizabeth, always anxious to promote every spirit of enterprise and bold adventure, granted these letters, and gave every encouragement to the expedition. The Company sent, this year, three vessels—one called the Swallow, in which Jenkinson embarked. They left Gravesend in May, and arrived at Colmogro, in the bay of St. Nicholas, in July. On arriving in Moscow, one of the Secretaries of State, who was unfriendly to Jenkinson, prevented his having access to the Emperor. However, after having been detained all the winter, the Emperor sent for him, and not only granted him permission to pass through Russia, but also gave him letters to different foreign princes through whose domi-

1561.

nions he might pass, and entrusted to him the management of some of his own private affairs.

On the 25th April, Jenkinson, after taking leave of the Emperor, left Moscow; and, taking boat on the Wolga, he arrived at Astrachan in July. Embarking on the Caspian, he touched at Derbent and at Shabran, where he unloaded his goods. The King of Hyrcania, hearing of his arrival, sent an escort to conduct him to his court, which he held in the city of Shamakey. He found the King living in the mountains, in tents, to avoid the heat. He received Jenkinson most kindly, and gave him an escort to Cashin, where the Sophy held his court, and which was thirty days' journey from Shamakey. In November, Jenkinson arrived at Cashin, where he had an audience with the Sophy, who, having questioned him as to his religious belief, dismissed him from his presence; and, through the intrigues of the Turkish Ambassador, he was detained till the March following, (1563,) when, through the friendship of the King of Hyrcania, whose son was at the court of Persia, he was allowed to depart. Jenkinson returned by the route he came, and arrived, in Moscow, in July, 1530. Soon after his arrival, he had an audience of the Emperor; who, after much conference with him, about the affairs he had committed to his charge, he said, " I perceive your good sense, and will " recompense you for it." Jenkinson answered,

1562.

1563.

that he heartily rejoiced his services were acceptable to his Highness; that all he had done was but his duty, and that he beseeched his Highness to continue his favour to the Russia Company, and to give them a new privilege more ample than the first—all which the Emperor immediately granted. Jenkinson, in his own narrative and words, writes, "Afterwards, having
" penned a brief note, how I meant to have the
" same privileges made, I repaired daily to the
" secretary to perfect the same, and obtained it
" under his Majesty's broad seal, which, at my
" coming away, I delivered to Mr. Thomas
" Glover, agent for the Company in Moscow;
" and so, having sojourned all that winter in
" Moscow, I departed thence the 28th June, by
" post, and coming to Colmogro, and so down
" to the sea-side, I embarked, in the Swallow, on

1564. " the 9th July; and, after great dangers of loss
" of ship, goods, and life, arrived at London,
" (God be praised,) the 28th September, 1564."

The Russia Company, always having in view the great object of discovering a route to China, and extending the commerce of England, directed their factors in Moscow, Thomas Alcock, George Wren, and Richard Cherrie, to make a journey into Persia. The report of this journey was made by Thomas Alcock, who wrote, as follows, to the Company. " On the 10th of May, 1563,
" we left Yaroslaw, and arrived at Astrachan in

" the end of July; in August we entered the
" Caspian Sea, and about the middle arrived at
" our port in Medea; and, on the 21st, we arrived
" at Shamakey, where King Obdowloun received
" us very kindly." In October they arrived at
Cashin. This party evinced so little judgement,
that no advantages were attained; and Alcock,
on his return, was murdered, as is supposed, by
robbers.

In the year 1565 a mission was sent to Persia, under the direction of Richard Johnson, Alexander Kitching, and Arthur Edwards, factors of the Russia Company.   1565.

This expedition left Astrachan the end of July, 1565; but, owing to contrary winds, they did not reach the destined Port, Nazavoe, till the 23d of August. On the 5th of September, the party arrived at Shamakey, where the king of Hyrcania received them with great kindness, inquiring much after Master Jenkinson. During their stay at his court the good king died, which was a great misfortune for the Company, and occasioned much trouble and difficulties to the party. They remained there the winter; and, in spring, Mr. Arthur Edwards, who had been sent on a special mission, by Mr. Richard Johnson, the Company's agent in Moscow, to the Shah of Persia, left Shamakey, and arrived at Cashin the end of May. He was well received by the Shah, who   1565.   1566.

granted great privileges and powers of trading to the Company.

Mr. Edwards, on his last mission, having communicated to the Company, that there was a great consumption and demand for cloth, and having received from the Shah a paper, or document, giving to the Company the privilege of trading, he, as agent to the Company, with Laurence Chapman, and other servants of the Russia Company, in July, 1568, left Yaroslaw, and, in August, arrived at a port called Bilbel, in the Caspian Sea. Here they did not find the Shah's letter of the use they expected; and they were obliged to sell their cloths at the prices the people put upon them. They left this place on camels, and arrived at Shamakey in September; thence they proceeded to a place called Ardouil, where they sold cloths at good prices. This place not being far from Tauris, the capital of Persia, Mr. Chapman was sent with an interpreter to that place; but he found the market so overstocked with cloths and kerseys, which had been brought thither from Aleppo, that he was only offered very low prices. Mr. Edwards proceeded on his mission to Cashin, where he was kindly treated; and the Company received new privileges, which were written on a parchment in azure and gold letters.

1568.

1566.   In the year 1566, Queen Elizabeth confirmed,

and secured, by act of parliament, the privileges of the charter of the Russia or Muscovy Company, naming it, " The Fellowship of English " Merchants for the Discovery of unknown " Lands."

In the year 1568 the Company sent Thomas Banister and Geofrey Ducket on a mission to Persia: they left Yaroslaw in July, and arrived at Astrachan in August. Crossing the Caspian Sea, the party arrived at Bilbel in October, from whence they went to Shamakey, where they remained the winter: and in April of the following year, 1569, they went to Ardouil, a place of great account, by reason of its being the sepulchre of the Persian Kings. Here they remained six months, but found little commerce, it being more frequented by noblemen and gentlemen than by merchants. The Shah Thomas sent a messenger to invite the party to Cashin. Mr. Ducket being unwell, could not go; but Mr. Banister did, and was well received; and the Shah granted great privileges to the Company. After remaining six months, Mr. Banister went to Tauris, where he found Mr. Ducket in good health.

Mr. Banister returned from Tauris to Shamakey, and then went four days' journey to Arrash, to purchase raw silks; but, owing to the unwholesome air and stagnated water, Mr. Banister, with Laurence Chapman, and some other

1568.

1569.

Englishmen, died. Mr. Ducket returned from Cashin to Shamakey, and went from thence to Cassan, a town of great traffic. Here they remained ten weeks; then returned to Bilbel, where

1573. they embarked, in May, 1573. On their passage they were attacked by Cossacks, who took their ship, and put the party into boats, in which they arrived at Astrachan. Mr. Ducket went to Moscow to lodge his complaints before the Emperor, who, pitying the great loss they had sustained by his own subjects, purchased such goods as they had remaining, (having recovered a part from the Cossacks,) and paid for them with ready money. They spent the winter in Moscow; and, purchasing such goods as suited the English market, they journeyed to St. Nicholas, where

1574. they embarked in August, and arrived, in October, in England.

1568. In the year 1568 the friendly intercourse and trade with Russia was nearly interrupted, the Czar having been much displeased with the conduct of the merchants residing in Moscow. The trade between Russia and Great Britain had become of great importance and value. The Czar had granted the Muscovy Company an exemption from all customs, with leave to transport their manufactures through his whole dominions, and transport them into Persia and Media by the Caspian Sea; whereas, the merchants of other nations were not allowed to trade beyond Moscow. With this permission, the Russia Company ventured to transport their goods in boats made of one entire tree, up the rivers to Vologda; from thence, in seven days, by land, to Yaroslaw, and then, in thirty days and nights, by the Volga to Astrachan. From Astrachan they crossed the Caspian Sea, and made their way through the vast Deserts of Hyrcania to Cashin, in Persia, in hopes, at length, to discover a route to China; but, by reason of the war between the Turks and Persians, and the robberies committed by these barbarians, the Russia Company was, at last, discouraged from pursuing the glorious enterprise.

Queen Elizabeth, always alive to the interests of the country, and anxious to arrange the differences between the Czar and the Russia Company, sent an embassy to Moscow in 1562. The Ambassador, who was sent on this important mission, was Thomas Randolph; he embarked, at Harwich, in a vessel, called the Harry, in June, and arrived at St. Nicholas in July. He arrived at Colmogro, about seventy-five miles from St. Nicholas, where he waited till a gentleman of the Court arrived to conduct him to Moscow, which he reached the end of September.

The Czar appeared to be at first much irritated; but, by the prudent conduct and good judgement of the Ambassador, he not only became pacified, but granted several new and important privileges to the Company, particularly as to the trade with Persia, and the endeavour to discover a route to China, which were confirmed by a personal alliance, for the concluding of which the Czar sent an Ambassador to the Queen: he accompanied Randolph to St. Nicholas, where they embarked and arrived in London in September. The Ambassador sent by the Czar, was Andrew Gregoriewitz Savin, who had a splendid retinue, according to the fashion of the country. He was received with great honours by the Russia Company, and most courteously by Queen Elizabeth. He exhibited a certain treaty which he desired the Queen to sign, which was done with this reserve, " as not interfering with treaties " made with other Princes." This so offended the Czar, that he began to treat the English with slights and affronts, and threatened to revoke their privileges. Before leaving Moscow, Mr. Randolph sent an expedition, under James Bassenden, to explore the coast eastwards from the River Pechora.

1569.

The displeasure of the Czar not having altogether subsided, the Russia Company petitioned Queen Elizabeth to send out an Ambassador, who might act in the double capacities of Ambassador from the Queen and agent from the Company.

The Ambassador chosen for this mission was

Mr. Anthony Jenkinson, who had before been intrusted with three special missions to Russia. The selection was most fortunate, for the Czar was so enraged with the Company and the Court of London, that, on Mr. Jenkinson's arrival, in July, 1571, at St. Nicholas, he was informed, 1571. the Czar was so sorely displeased with the British Government, that his proceeding to Moscow might be attended with great personal dangers to himself. Mr. Jenkinson did not arrive in Moscow till the February following, 1572; and it 1572. was only in the month of March that the Emperor granted him an audience. On presenting his credentials and letters from Queen Elizabeth, the Emperor was in great wrath; but, on the the judicious explanations and courteous manners of the Ambassador, his anger was appeased; and, at another audience, he informed Mr. Randolph that all his prayers for the Company would be acceded to, and new and greater privileges granted to the Company. Thus was the Russia Company perfectly established under the protection of Queen Elizabeth, and the Czar Iwan Basiliewich, and a perfect friendship confirmed between the two kingdoms.

Purchas, who published, in 1625, a Collection of Travels and Voyages, which he called "Purchas his Pilgrims," gives to the Russia Company the merit of having fitted out the expedition, commanded by Martin Frobisher, and of having granted license and leave to Sir Humphrey Gilbert, in his first expedition, and writes as follows: "The Muscovy Company having "sought for the north-east passage by sea, and "finding such great and insurmountable dif- "ficulties, resolved to make trial if the north- "west part would not afford a passage to the "Indies, which was the first and main scope of

1576. "their northern discoveries; and, in the year "1576, they sent forth Sir Martin Frobisher "with ten barks, who, coming into the height "of sixty-two, found a great inlet, now known "by the name of Frobisher's Straits, into which "he put himself, and sailed sixty leagues with "a main land on each side, and so for that year "returned."

1577. The following year he made a second voyage to that place, purposely to load himself with a kind of ore, which the year before he had found there, and gave hopes, by the colour, to yield gold, and being laden with some quantity returned.

1578. The succeeding year, having made trial of that ore, and finding it not to fall out according to his expectations, he was furnished out to proceed further in those Straits, and, entering therein, made way as far as he thought fit, and then returned, having first taken possession, in the name of Queen Elizabeth, who called the place Meta Incognita.

In 1580, the Russia Company, desirous to make another attempt to discover the north-east passage to China, fitted out two small barks,—the George of 40 tons, Arthur Pitt, and the William of 20 tons, Charles Jackman. The expedition arrived at Waigatz, and passed through the Straits; sailed along the coast of Nova Zembla, and the north of Russia, and the country of the Samoiedes, as far as the ice would permit therein, and finding no possibility of passing, by reason of the ice, they gave up the attempt. The George arrived safe in England in the same year, but the William was lost and was never more heard of. Thus ended this unsuccessful voyage, and the Company, thus discouraged, did not for many years after attempt this passage.

1580.

The trade of the Russia Company had become so important, and of such magnitude, that, in 1582, they fitted out nine vessels; and, from the instructions given to the Commander of this fleet, it appears a larger force than was usually sent out, for the double purpose of defence and of trade. The instructions having been to this effect—" Forasmuch as the number of ships we
" intend sending in this fleet to St. Nicholas is
" greater than usual, it having come to our
" knowledge that you may be met with such
" who may assault you with force and violence

1582.

"as enemies we have thought it good to appoint an Admiral and Vice-Admiral to the command."

1583. In 1583, by the leave and admittance of the Muscovy Company, Sir Humphry Gilbert went out for the discovery of the north part of Terra Florida, came into the great River of Canada, called St. Laurence, took possession of the country, and settled the government of the fishery there, which is so well known at this time.

1585. In the year 1585, Master John Davis was furnished out, at Dartmouth, with two barks, for the discovery of the north-west passage, came into the height of 66°, plyed along the coast, observed the probability of a passage, and in the end of the year returned.

1586. In the year following he went out again, in the further discovery thereof; found a great inlet between 55° and 56° latitude, which gave him great hopes of a passage; traded with the people there, and so returned.

1587. In the year 1587 he made a third voyage to those places, followed his course to the north and north-west to the latitude 67°, having the Continent, (which he called America,) on the west side, and Greenland (which he named Desolation) on the east; and going to the height of 86 degrees, the passage enlarged so that he could not see the western shore; thus he continued in latitude 73°, in a great sea free from ice, of an unmeasurable depth; and having despatched two ships, for the purpose of fishing, he returned home. This passage was named Fretum Davis, and bears the name of the discoverer—Davis Straits—to this day. Thus the discovery of the northern seas proceeded on, from time to time, by the endeavour and charge of the Muscovia Company, until they had particularly discovered the lands, coasts, islands, straits, ravins, bays, rivers, or other places therein, and measured every part thereof, by thus often tracing to and fro, as may be seen by their reports and journals, lodged at the High Court of the Admiralty.

The Emperor having, in the year before, sent an ambassador to the court of London, Queen Elizabeth, on his return, resolved on sending a special embassy to Moscow; and, for this purpose, selected Sir Jerome Bowes, a gentleman of her court: he, with forty followers, left Gravesend in June, and arrived at St. Nicholas in July.

On his arrival, he found that the Dutch, by intrigue, had made powerful attempts to dislodge the Russia Company, and had gained over, by bribery, three of the chief counsellors of the Emperor. The Ambassador, on his first audience, by reason of these intrigues, was coldly received by the Czar, who stated he did not consider the Queen of England as equal to himself.

Sir Jerome Bowes, by a spirited answer, and using great caution and discretion, coupled with firmness, so worked upon the Emperor that he was received with great favour, and the Emperor granted all his demands, and confirmed, and even increased the privileges he had before granted to the Russia Company; all which was signed and sealed, and was to have been delivered to him on his next coming to court, when, unhappily, the Emperor died of a surfeit in April, 1584, having reigned fifty-four years. On the death of the Emperor, the chief counsellors, who had been bribed by the Dutch, coming into power, not only refused to deliver the Grant of Privileges which had been signed by the late Emperor, but confined him as a prisoner in his own house. After some time, he was brought before the new Emperor, who treated him with great indignity, and ordered him to leave the country before the coronation. His journey to St. Nicholas was attended with much personal risk: he embarked from thence in August, and arrived in England in September. On the death of Iwan Basieliwich, his son, Pheodor Iwanowich, was proclaimed Emperor, and was crowned, with great solemnity, in June, 1584. After the ceremony of the coronation, the Emperor sent for Mr. John Horsey; but a

1584.

famous merchant from the Netherlands, Mr. De Wall, endeavoured to take precedence. The Emperor, observing the altercation, desired Mr. Horsey first to advance, who presented the offerings of the British merchants, which the Emperor received most graciously; and made the assurance that, for the sake of his sister, Queen Elizabeth, he would be a gracious lord to her merchants in as ample a manner as his father ever had been. Not long after the coronation, Mr. Horsey was sent from the Emperor on a message to the Queen of England: he departed from Moscow in September, and travelling over land, delivered his letter to the Queen, who forthwith commanded him to repass into Russia, where he arrived, by sea, in April, 1586; and, on reaching Moscow, he was so well received by the Emperor, that he obtained for the Russia Company such extended and great privileges as were never before granted. 1586.

In the year 1588, Queen Elizabeth sent an ambassador, Doctor Giles Fletcher, a Doctor of Civil Law, into the country of Russia, as well to treat with the new Emperor about league and amity, as with his father, as well as for re-establishing and reducing into order the trade of the Russia Company. The Ambassador, on his first arrival, was not well received; yet, in the end, he obtained of the Emperor many important conditions and privileges, and was 1588.

courteously and honourably dismissed, receiving, from the Emperor, a letter to the Lord High Treasurer, Burleigh, dated in July, 1590.

In the years 1591 and 1592, many letters were interchanged between the courts of Russia and England on the subject of privileges, grants, &c. for the Russia Company: and, in the year 1596, after much negotiation and prayer, the Emperor Pheodor Iwanowich confirmed the former privileges granted to the Russia Company, and added to and extended them very considerably.

1597. In March, 1597, Pheodor Iwanowich died, and was succeeded by his son, Boris Pheodorowich, who confirmed the privileges and grants given by the former Emperor.

The Russia Company, although discouraged by the want of success which had hitherto attended their endeavours to discover a passage to China, either by the NE or NW, still never lost sight of an undertaking which was of so much importance to the great interests of the nation, and of the world at large; and, in 1602. the year 1602, they resolved to send out an expedition to attempt a passage, by sea, by the NW. For this purpose, they fitted out two fly-boats, one of seventy, the other of sixty tons burthen, with two years' provisions, under the command of Mr. George Weymouth. They left Gravesend in May, reaching the latitude of

69°; they met with so much ice, frost, and fog, that the sailors were discouraged, and refused to proceed; whereupon, they shaped their course to England, where they arrived in September.

In the year 1603, Queen Elizabeth died: in this year, the Russia Company sent out a small vessel, called the Grace, under the command of Stephen Bennett, to sail to those parts north of the North Cape: he landed on Cherry Island, where he killed many sea-horses, and brought home some lead ore.

1603.

On the accession of James the First, an embassy was sent to the court of Moscow; and Sir Thomas Smith, Governor of the Russia Company, with Sir J. Chaloner and Sir William Wray, were selected for the important mission. The embassy was most graciously received; and the Emperor Boris Phoedorowich confirmed all the former privileges granted to the Company.

1604.

In March, in the following year, the ambassador took his leave. Before embarking at St. Nicholas, which he did in May, the news of the death of the Emperor, and the accession to the throne of the Emperor Demetrius Iwanowich was communicated by a special messenger, who was the bearer of a letter from the Emperor to the King of England.

1605.

In the following year, the Emperor granted new privileges to the Russia Company, the grant

1606.

or charter of which was sent to England by Mr. Oliver Lysset, one of the agents of the Russia Company.

In this year, Demetrius Iwanowich was murdered; having, before his death, acknowledged that he was an impostor, and had no right to the throne which he had assumed. He was succeeded by Wassiley Iwanowich, who sent over Mr. John Merick, one of the factors of the Russia Company, on a special mission, entrusting to him a letter to the King of England, and the Grant of Privileges to the Russia Company.

This Emperor was succeeded by Michael Phoedorowich Romanoff, who gave a charter, or grant, to the Russia Company, confirming all former, and granting new privileges. This charter is granted to Sir Thomas Smith, Sir John Merick, Governor, Consuls, and Court of Assistants of the Russia Company.

1608. In the year 1608, the Russia Company despatched the Hopewell, William Hudson master, to discover the Pole; where it appeareth, by his Journal, that he came to the height of 81 degrees, where he gave names to certain places upon the Continent of Greenland, namely, Whale Bay, Hakluyt's Headland, and, being stopped by ice, returned home; and, in sailing back, he discovered an island in 71 degrees, which he named Hudson's Touches. Hence it is to be seen that the Russia Company having, by often resort and employments in these parts, observed a great number of sea-horses at Cherry Island, likewise a multitude of whales, which shewed themselves upon the coast of Greenland, they first applied themselves to the killing of morses, which they continued to do from year to year, from 1604 to 1609, by sending out one or two vessels, which were commanded by Captain Thomas Wilden. In the year 1609, Thomas Wilden, with whom was joined in commission Thomas Edge, took formal possession, for the Russia Company, of the Cherry Island, which was remarkable and important to the great interests of the Company, as James the First afterwards, in consequence, granted to the Russia Company the exclusive privilege of the whale-fishery.

1609

In the year 1610, the Russia Company fitted out two vessels, under the command of Jonas Poole, for the purposes of northern discovery; but it does not appear that the expedition reached a very high latitude, and it returned, without effecting any new discovery, in the same year.

1610.

THE ESTABLISMENT

OF THE

WHALE - FISHERY.

1611. The Muscovy or Russia Company, weighing all the accounts of the northern navigation and the great returns and advantages to the country which might arise from a well-regulated whale-fishery, in the year 1611, sent out two vessels, the Mary-Margaret, Thomas Edge, commander, and Elizabeth, James Poole, well provided for the expedition. On board of the vessels were put an unusual number of men, that there might be no want of hands, and in each were sent three Biscayans, to manage the fish. These were the first ships sent from England upon this employment, though the expedition itself was most unfortunate, one of the vessels having been lost, with the whole crew, and the other also lost, but some of the people escaped.

In 1612, the Russia Company sent out two vessels, under the command of Thomas Edge, which were very successful; on this expedition, Thomas Edge, meeting with a Dutch vessel, ordered her off the fishing-ground.

In 1613, the Russia Company sent out seven vessels, under the command of Thomas Edge and Benjamin Johnson, and, having received the king's patent, under the broad seal of England, to forbid all strangers, and others, to use the Coast of Greenland, they ordered off fifteen vessels,—two Dutch, four English, and the rest French, Spanish, &c. This expedition discovered Hope Island to the eastward.

In the following year, 1614, James the First confirmed the Charter given to the Russia Company; and, further, granted to the Company the Right and exclusive Grant of " the Whale-" Fishery."

1614.

" That, whereas the Russia Company did dis-
" cover and take possession of Greenland, Cherry-
" Island, and did raise there the British stan-
" dard, we do grant to this Fellowship and Com-
" pany the exclusive privilege of fishing for
" Whales. Signed, at Westminster, the 11th
" year of our reign in England, France, and Ire-
" land, and the 46th in Scotland." In this year the Company fitted out several vessels, not only for the purpose of the Whale-Fishery, but, likewise, for the object of discovery; these ships were under the command of Thomas Edge and Benjamin Johnson. This year the Dutch, being stronger than the English, and convoyed by three men of war, refused to return, but their fishery was unsuccessful. The Company made but a poor voy-

age, the ships having returned half-laden. This year the Company discovered, northward, as high as 80°, some islands to the eastward of Greenland, in a vessel commanded by William Raffer and Robert Fotherby. In 1615 Thomas Edge and Benjamin Johnson were again despatched, but not being strong enough to drive off the Dutch and Danish vessels which they found fishing, they returned with half-laden vessels. A vessel, under the command of Thomas Fotherby, reached as high 80°; and, in latitude 71°, discovered an island, which he named Sir Thomas Smith's Island, after the Governor of the Russia Company.

1616. In 1616 eight vessels were sent out under the command of Thomas Edge: this was a most successful expedition, and they returned with full ships. In this voyage Edge-Island was discovered.

1617. In 1617 the Company was very successful, having brought home 2000 tons of oil and killed 1500 sea-horses.

1618. In 1618 a new Company, consisting of English, Scotch, and Zealanders, procured a grant, or license, for fishing, which opposition would have been so injurious to the interests of the Russia Company that they were obliged to purchase out this Company. In this year the Russia Company made an agreement with the East-Land Company to join stocks in this trade, who sent out fifteen ships, under the command of Thomas Edge; and they, having been attacked and dispersed by the Dutch, whom they found in great force, this voyage was most unsuccessful, and greatly discouraged the two Companies.

In the year 1619 the Russia and East-Land Companies sent out nine ships, under the command of Thomas Edge, but this voyage was more disastrous and unfortunate than the former, and so disheartened the Russia Company that they were no longer desirous to continue these adventures, but were willing to grant licenses, &c. to those who might wish to embark in the undertaking. 1619.

In the year 1620 the worthy and famous Merchant-Adventurers, all Brethren of the Russia Company, namely, Ralph Freeman, Benjamin Discrowe, George Stuart, with Captain Thomas Edge, pitying the downfall of so worthy a traffic and nursery of mariners, in which yearly so many poor landsmen received comfort, at their own charge, compounded with the Company, and took the trade into their own hands. In this year they sent out seven ships, under the command of William Riley, but they were not rewarded with that success which such spirited conduct well entitled them to. 1620.

In 1621 these spirited Adventurers fitted out eight vessels, which made a successful voyage, bringing home 1200 tons of oil.

In 1622 the same Adventurers fitted out nine ships, eight for the fisheries and one for discovery, which was wrecked off the coast of Greenland. The rest of the ships returned home safe, but brought poor cargoes; and so great was the opposition from the Dutch and Danes, that, for a long time, the Greenland fishery was not pursued by the English.

THE END.

MARCHANT, PRINTER, INGRAM-COURT.

Printed by Libri Plureos GmbH in Hamburg, Germany